FAILURE IS NOT AN OPTION

By Nancy D. Parsley

2016

FAILURE IS NOT AN OPTION

Saving faith

Faith is a gift God gives us because he is saving us

(Ephesians 2:8, NLV)

PROLOGUE

<u>My Journey Towards Faith</u>

If I were to take a comprehensive look at when faith became a frequent word or action in my daily life it was probably eight to ten years ago. This was a time when I resigned myself to the sheer fact that, in some areas of my life, things were not happening the way that they needed to.

This took quite a bit of surrender on my part, to try a new approach.

Learning how to view things differently and change how I had gone about my life for over thirty years, did not have to be such a grind. After all, the good news for me, was the realization that one does not have to continue doing the same behavior, just because it's what you're accustomed to doing.

This was my initial enlightenment, and a big revelation which made all of the subsequent changes possible. Over the next three years, I worked on a program of behavior change. That program included others who succeeded in changing some patterns of behavior that contributed to low self-esteem and a poor quality of life. These relationships became life changing. They allowed me to grow socially and build significant relationships as well. I also started to pray and take stock in the knowledge of the creator; God.

    One of the main things I had to change was how my thoughts would condemn me. I don't think my worst enemy would be as wicked to me as I was to myself. I really did not know how to be kind to myself, and in return struggled to be kind to those around me. It starts with self and expands outward from there. I found it really is true that you cannot give away to others what you do not possess.

A return to Church was my next milestone, not that I totally stopped going. Even though I had been attending, its impact had been minimal in my life. But, what was I really looking for in going anyways? Clearly, it was not completely clear to me at the time. When I listened to the Pastor talk about being a new person in Christ, I was listening with intent as he discussed (Matthew 9:17 NIV), "Neither do men pour new wine into old wineskins. If they do, the skins will burst, the wine will run out and the wineskins will be ruined. No, they pour new wine into new wineskins, and both are preserved."

Understanding this scripture did not come easy. It's not that i did not understand it intellectually, but in a heartfelt way, I did not grasp it. You have to ask yourself, "Am I a new person in Christ?" or, "Do I just have new knowledge, and the prospects of being a new person is exciting?" It's okay to be at that place, because I was. I had to go through the ropes course, if you will, to learn how to be a different person.

That is what it's like when you learn new behavior, someone teaches you, and that is because you are in agreement to have them teach you. Otherwise you will remain in the old patterns of relating until you become ready and willing. In other words, life gets pretty stagnant. A person's journey is a story. It is based on their personal, heartfelt, experiences. It is not right or wrong.

That same year, while attending this church, was a time of preparation. I was not only challenged to hear, read, and think about God's word, I was challenged to put it into the daily workings of my life. This was a huge difficulty! It takes, what it takes, and when you reach a new level or milestone you know it because it gets easier.

Having a changed heart and a changed mind comes out into your life and the way you interact with family, friends, and co-workers. Mastering this is a test in your journey to faith and transformation. Many levels follow as God takes us from place to place or from glory to glory.

Understanding the Ten Commandments and their application in our life is beautiful and necessary. Evolving for God's higher purpose is like attending the best Ivy League University, while we are not yet college material. We often fall short of who God wants us to be. We often don't even know his calling for our life. It can be easy to veer in a direction opposite of God's leading. Yes, his leading is there, but we are too busy to watch and listen. If you are reading this book, God is saying, "It's time!"

1   Front and Center

We walked down a hallway that lead us through a door and into a theater type room with a huge stage. The stage was raised up pretty high, and I remember thinking, "this must be something spectacular". It was our first time attending a non-denominational church. We normally attended catholic service. The seats filled up quickly. My husband Len choose one of the aisles towards the back, and of course, the two seats on the end. Between his weak bladder and my social anxiety, we could make an escape that would be less noticeable. We could then hop in our car and be off to Bob Evans or elsewhere for a well-deserved breakfast. Erin, our fourteen-year-old at the time didn't care much, as long as she could get out as soon as possible.

In the midst of the age of rebellion, what were these two adults that passed on this very seed going to do? I bloomed into adulthood late and was still blooming in my forties. Len caught on earlier than me and realized it was the career that counted the most. So, he signed on for the Navy. This was good considering he was irresponsible and kind of a knucklehead at the time. Before he left for the Navy, he made sure to get his girlfriend pregnant, got married, and moved to Florida where the Navy placed him for the time being.

I could see the worship team heading onto the stage. "Worship team" was not a term I knew before we attended. Several instruments and vocalists made up the band, who were young to middle age adults. All ages were included. The music went straight to my heart and I experienced a sense of peace. I joined in singing and tried to catch onto the words as quickly as possible.

I knew that we had arrived at a place that would help us to make the changes we had longed for. It was a place we had never been before. Twenty minutes had past. The band left from the stage and the pastor started to speak. We listened intently, receiving every new word. It was a message that was truly significant. I was inspired.

Len listened for a while, but his heart meds tended to make him drowsy when he sat down, I looked over and nudged him gently to wake him. "Wake up," I whispered, in the usual commanding way. His eyes darted about and then finally back to the Pastor. I knew Len struggled, but an uncomfortable feeling would well up in me when I looked over to find him asleep. I often thought, "what if he started to snore?" I would be mortified. Thankfully, it never did happen, although nudging was a regular ritual for Sunday service.

I tended to be really uptight about getting to service on time. It really went back to my childhood and Sunday morning mass. Father McFadden's bald head would turn beet red as he chastised the parishioners who came in late. On occasion, that would be all of the Reilly family (my family). My Dad would be livid. He could not stand to tolerate Father's temper. My guess is that these two Irishmen had something in common.

My fear of judgment and rejection would stir up emotional chaos. Len would sometimes look at me with a puzzled expression on his face.

Empathy seemed to elude Len, and I wondered if all men were emotionally stunted at about the age of twelve. Yes, God had his work cut-out for him between the two of us! Then, of course, there was Erin and Trish (our girls), but i'll get to them later.

The worship team ended the service. The music was beautiful, the message inspiring, and we were now off to a white canopy tent that could house at least a couple hundred people. Len and I went straight for the coffee. We moseyed about getting a glimpse of various literatures. We were encouraged to fill-out a card with name, phone and possible areas we wanted to help out.

Len stood drinking his coffee while I started to talk with a lady at one of the tables. I was anxious to connect with people and hoped to make friends via a bible study. I was often guilty of jumping in with both feet, then finding it was not what I thought. I had a habit of getting in over my head.

Len had a better approach, he would just hang back, and say hello to those walking by. No, I couldn't do the subtle approach! Why was I so needy? I might as well have had a big sign that said "LIKE ME!" This is probably the reason why it was a rough go for me to make friends. I wanted to be accepted and was terrified to be rejected. I swapped numbers with the lady and off we went.

Breakfast at Bob Evans was good, all things considered, other than Erin's, "When are we leaving"? When are we going home?" I thought that stopped at a younger age. Well, remember the parental trend of late bloomers. Need I say more?

The following week we received an e-newsletter from the church about up and coming activities. It also stated, that, if we were attending service on Sunday we needed to sit front and center, leaving outside seats for new people. Of course, I found that uncomfortable, because I thought I was still a new person and not ready to move on to the next level.

To recap, Len had heart disease and, an emotional mindset of a twelve-year-old and I wanted to be highly involved but was thwarted by often rather severe social anxiety. So off we go to family issues…

2   Focus on the Family

Yes! We all have family issues to some extent or another. It can be hard to admit your issues. It is hard not to be in denial out of fear you will say something too strange, and someone might consider you crazy. This is not how I see myself or us. A little depression, a little wine, a little OCD doesn't really hurt, does it? It must've been the cumulative effect that went out into our life and rendered us ineffective.

The fact that Len and I were, from the children's age of twelve, unable to be effective parents, put us in a serious quandary. We heard talk about putting parents in jail with their children. "Oh, please God, we really have not been that bad." You wonder how bad it might get when you have lost control over your children. What might they do next? We needed and wanted to be enlightened. We needed to grow in faith and to understand what wonderful thing our creator made us for. Without knowing who we were in Christ, how could we teach our children their identity in this world.

So, for me, a strict Catholic family upbringing and education, leaves me with a few good memories. Mostly reflections of those cherished moments with our beloved nuns. Eight siblings provided for good camaraderie, but it also calls for an excellent referee. This is what we had only part time. The remainder of the time, we got the snot beat out of us if we did not follow the hierarchical chain of command. I had four older sisters. Needless to say, it was far and few between when I got my way. Oh, you could get your way, and then get paid back when no referee was around. You learn to survive by suppressing your thoughts and feelings.

Do you remember (table rosé) the blank slate, that's what you stayed if you wanted to be out of the line of trouble. I pretty much kept reeled in until I turned thirteen, and then all bets were off. I was in rebellion! I was running rampant and I had an opinion for everything.

Then one day everything changed when I met-up with an interesting guy. His name was Raymond. Raymond was fresh out of college and looking for adventure. As Cat Stevens said, "He was on the road to find out," and so was I. After two weeks he informed me that he was moving to San Diego. He asked me if I was interested. I had waited for this moment since high school graduation and it was finally the opportunity I had waited for! So, I decided to go with him.

My oldest sister Sarah, who was my second parent figure after my mother, was sure that the family would never see me again. Pillaged, murdered, and left for dead in a ditch were possibilities in the creative minds of the Reilly clan. Creativity ran rampant in the Reilly family. I had a few thoughts of my own, a few thoughts and reflections about my childhood sanctuary. My favorite place in nature was the beloved orchard near our house. It was conveyed in a poem I called "Wet Grass Sneakers":

One morning I awoke to the birds chirping.
I dressed myself, put my sneakers on and went outside.

The sky was not sunny yet and the grass was misty and wet.

I jumped on my swing, up, up high, almost to the sky,

and then grabbed a leaf from the tree top.

Slow, slower, slowing down,

my sneakers skid me to a stop.

Now for something special I really like a lot,

dangling my head back,

looking up at the sky for what seemed to be a very long time.

Swaying, swaying is the sky moving too?

What is next for me to do?

Swinging is fun but it is time for me to run off to the orchard.

There are apple trees and sometimes bees that like this fruit a lot.

What a surprise I see!

A patch of baby red strawberries,

grapes hanging from a vine and,

look! Look! Blackberries too!

all dripping with morning dew

Come run in the orchard with me through the misty grass and many fruit trees.

Butterflies on blossoms, Caterpillars crawling and birds flying up high,

I can find them all, why don't you try?

Being seen and not heard, and keeping my head down to avoid getting in a sibling matter was less than desirable. The reflection lasted momentarily. I was determined to find my own peaceful place of escape. I left with a couple pairs of jeans. It was a minimalists move. The grand prim- per, that unloaded the entire closet of my assets just to locate the right outfit for my hostess job at a local restaurant, was changing the tides.

This was a duo move. An agreement was made with friends of Raymond's that we would drive one of their cars. It had a small U-Haul trailer attached which housed Raymond's motorcycle which was our source of transportation. Off we went with a final destination of San Diego.

Ten years after the move, back in my hometown and single, I met Lenny. Len was so refreshing to me. He was a different type of person than I was accustomed to and that was a good thing! He appeared adult for all intents and purposes. He wore khaki pants and a light blue, button down, oxford type shirt. He had what sounded to me to be an important occupation. All I knew is that he didn't want to change his name to "Free Cloud" or keep a pet owl in the house. That was a good thing too!

His family was also very refreshing to me. They were not the "Quiet! What will the neighbors think," type. They were the "quietly let the neighbors think what they like type!" Refreshing! Refreshing! Refreshing! Len was talkative but could be quiet in his own way.

Len could not be more of a gentleman. He was raised in the South and spoke with a slight accent. I would tease him over the years about his unique choice of words. Only to find out after sixteen years of marriage that to, "cut-off the lights", is actually a southern expression, and not just an alien expression that Len came-up with.

After we married, we came into agreement that I would have his baby and be the stay at home mom, and he would bring home the bacon. Since Raymond and I previously had a baby girl, this would be my second child. Raymond was never present for her life, since the life flight helicopter he was on while working as a nurse, crashed. He was killed instantly, about four years after the move. I was stunned and probably still in shock a few years later when I met Len, with a beautiful girl, who very much favored her Dad. So, what could be more appropriate? A beautiful plan evolved.

Shortly after we married, Trish and I moved to the south to start a new life and expand our family. This did not happen without protest by Trish, since she was attached to her Aunt Sarah and the place where we lived. "Besides, who was used to the Dad guy being around and what purpose could he possibly serve?"

This would be a contention over the next few years for her and all the family, even with the addition of her little sister Erin. Len and I did everything that was suggested by anyone in the "know". Get her a small gift to usher in this new event, let her hold her baby sister from the first moment we arrive home. We even have a special video "Trish giving Erin a tour of her new home." She was in the limelight, important, and loved. What went wrong?

Erin was healthy, happy, and thriving. Len came home to announce the possibility that he might be getting a transfer to Europe for three years. Needless to say I was excited but anxious about moving to such a faraway country. After all, my family never travelled farther than Michigan, from Ohio. Most of my entire family remained in our hometown. A few weeks later it was confirmed that we would relocate overseas.

3   NO ROOM FOR WIMPS!

Len and I had been married for about two years. How can I convey this to a man who has been beaten up and starved in boot camp, had a previous marriage with two children that ended in tragedy, worked the streets of the inner city as a police officer, and worked two jobs while he went to college mostly on the GI bill? He was a loving man to an extent but I could tell there was no room here for wimps.

Unfortunately, I was one, and he was really unaware of just how much of a wimp I was. Little did he know he was married to a fragile person, a shell at best? I had such a small amount of confidence, but I loved my children with a vengeance. Len would say, "I feel sorry for the person who gets in between you and the kids!" It was true. The intense passion for what I would say, especially in defense of my children, could make most a little uneasy. It took me a while, but I eventually learned to be calmer in the midst of the storm. God has really had his work cut out for him. Len was good at change and seemed to take it with a stride.

On January 1, 1993, Len was visiting with one of the neighbors enjoying some oysters and a beer. I could see him from the window at a glance, as I stuck my family's traditional New Year's meal in the oven. Pork roast and sauerkraut was for my side of the family tradition. Len's family favorites were greens and hopping johns. I'm not going to tell you what I thought when I became aware that, according to Len, we needed some of each meal to celebrate it right. So, Rice and black-eyed peas it was. Yippee!

Our meal cooking in the oven, I went out to greet the neighbors and join Len in the celebration. When I looked at Len, his face looked like paste, like pallor. This knowledge was fresh in my mind because of a recently completed CPR course, taken a few months ago, in preparation for Erin's birth. He said he was not feeling too well and I suggested he come in the house and lay down a bit. He did, but the symptoms got worse and he developed pain in his arm along with squeezing in his chest." Len, I'm going to call an ambulance," I told him. This is what I needed to do. Of course, he said, "no, just call my brother." I knew better but I went ahead and called his brother to take him to the hospital.

This would prove to be a slow ride for Len since his brother drives like he is ninety. After about ten minutes they arrived at the ER. Len and his brother walked into the hospital and Len told the clerk he thought he was having a heart attack.

They quickly sat him down and took his vital signs. His signs were seriously impaired and they had him head back into the ER where he promptly had a Cardiac arrest. I was still at home with the kids and calling my sitter when the hospital called and told me Len had a heart attack and they had revived him.

I can only explain it as the feeling I had when Raymond was killed and the Paramedics came to my house. I heard a knock on the door at 2:30 AM. It was Winnie, a local Paramedic, who traveled twenty miles from the city, and up to the small mountain town where we lived. I opened the door half in a daze, since I was in a pretty deep sleep. Winnie proceeded to tell me that the helicopter from the hospital had crashed. I waited to hear her continue, "no one survived," She said. Tears started to fill her eyes. I said, "Raymond?" She said, "Melanie, no one survived." It took me this period of time to realize what she was telling me. I felt a quick pulse of tears come to my eyes. I backed up until I reached the sofa and flopped down like a rag doll.

A warm feeling of numbness came over me. Also, the reason I was feeling somewhat sick and incoherent came to my mind. I was pregnant. Wow, life was not really real right now. The pregnancy test Ray and I took a couple of days ago was negative. I knew now I was pregnant, but he didn't. Life ends, life begins. This is not real right now. So, a similar theme was happening again. I did eventually grieve for Raymond's death. I had Trish, and fell in love with her instantly. Birth was an amazing event although, I found myself alone. It had to be a God thing. I knew that, even in the days of little faith.

But was Len going to be okay? I was almost getting a sense of indignation about this event that just happened to Len. "Oh, I just gave birth a couple of months ago and now you are checking out?" was my thought. He was alive that is what really mattered. I hurried off to the ER to meet with Len and the doctor not able to get a picture of what I would see when I got there.

Len spent some time in the hospital recuperating. I would visit him daily, but for some reason, I didn't want to be there. I had a woman that helped me with the kids when I had to visit Len. I would often have a couple glasses of wine before or after I went. He lay there at the mercy of the hospital staff and had a study that would determine what type of medicine he needed to take. This was frightening because it caused the heart to beat fast and almost out of control.

I felt angry and gyped like once before. Married life seemed to be elusive. I was afraid for

Trish and Erin. I was in terror. It was so hard for me to believe that the biggest wimp in town needed to be stronger than anyone I knew.

Most of the people I knew still lived in my hometown. They had the same friends and not much in life appeared to be changing for them. I was in survival mode. I did not wonder how well I was dealing with all of this. Let's just say a bottle of wine became my best friend. The drinking just filled in the gaps for Len's absence, not that I didn't care for the kids, I loved them a great deal. When Felicia watched them, I found my best friend. I became good at being high on wine and taking care of business, but like all good things they eventually come to an end.

4   Like a Timex Watch

A couple weeks later Len returned home from his stay in the hospital. He was a little pale looking but what can you expect after a near death experience, no actually a death experience. He told me all about it. You have to understand that Len is, to me, a very black and white person. What I say couldn't sound too, you know, cosmic or out of the realm of practicality. Otherwise, he would start being critical or not listen.

So, to hear this experience that he had the afternoon of his heart attack, was different. His heart stopped beating. He described the peaceful presence that he knew was with him as calm and reassuring. This presence conveyed to him the need for him to return to his wife and daughter. He saw an image of me and the girls. Shortly after he opened his eyes, many nurses, doctors, and others were around him. He was back and so was his heart.

A little bit of a different Len today, no cigarettes according to the Doc, unless he wanted to die in about a year. When I picked Len up at the hospital and handed him the same shirt that he had on that day, the cigarettes were still in the top pocket of his oxford shirt. Len felt the crinkle of the cig pack. His arm, and shirt in hand, jutted out towards me as he turned his head away. It was serious. If he continued to smoke, he would not live long. Len was very addicted. When we first met, I remember he had to leave the movie to have one. That's a serious addiction. Len enjoyed recuperating and spending time with the baby and Trish. It was good to be alive and home.

Somehow that sense of resentment seemed to linger for me. I wanted to overcome it all. I realized that I had better give up the smoking habit also. Leaving the house for a while and sitting in a mall parking lot to have a cigarette, got old quickly. I felt so bad to smoke in front of him. So, the challenge was on. In my home town plenty of teens and young adults did not smoke and neither of my parents smoked. It made it a little harder to understand why my siblings and I smoked.

Len and I both had "good" upbringings. I'm not suggesting our families were really healthy. They all had their own issues. I learned of much worse environments as I lived my adult life. What I thought was so bad, i realized, could have been much worse.

I went through frequent periods of counseling as an adult. Mainly to look at my issues and figure out why I was so messed up emotionally. Len thought he was always right and that was a big trigger for me. That played on my emotions a lot. We eventually had moments we could apply humor to some of our past conflicts. Len always said that I was already a counselor since I analyzed him for years. I would respond with, "If I had the money for all the sessions we had, we'd be pretty well off." The sarcasm and humor was our way to get through the tense times.

    Len's health post cardiac arrest was good but not without other illness. The following year we made that move to Europe, but it wasn't too long before we found out that he had a cancerous tumor on one of his kidneys. This made it necessary for us to travel back to the states for its removal. My sister was married to a doctor briefly and it was a good benefit since he hooked us up with a great specialist.

My old house, in the town where I grew up, now belonged to my sister. It was vacant since she was married just a few short months before. I loved the neighborhood since admiring it when I was a teenager. My best friend from middle school lived close to this area by the lake. We would walk around the neighborhoods visiting friends, jumping in the lake, or enjoying the snow in the winter months. It was awesomely beautiful in the snow. It would shower down like big cotton balls. There would be a blanket of silence, except for the giggles of girls venturing over to the latest popular boy's house. She was an awesome friend for me, who was very shy. She was outgoing and bubbly, always looking for a good laugh.

I feasted on all of these sweet memories while we were in my hometown. I had often wondered what I would be like if I had endured what Len had in his life. I know I had withstood less and been devastated emotionally more than he had. He lost his wife and two kids in a tragic house fire. God knew what he was doing when he joined us together. We were two heartbroken people trying to find peace in the world.

Len's operation went well and after recuperating for a couple of weeks, we were on our way back to Europe. I frequently tell Len he is like a Timex watch; he just keeps on ticking. I know it's vintage and corny, but he really has been blessed with a resiliency that most of us would find unusual. Even with all of my appreciation for Len's recovery, I continued to experience an underlying resentment that was fueled, by my frequent friend, alcohol.

4   Via Roma

There is much to be said about a place that inspires the senses and the spirit. A place where taste buds are tempted and then satisfied with the sweetness of strawberries, peaches, and blackberries. Then, to be plunged into the tart and forbidden fruit of the green unripe apple. What compelled us to partake of this fruit until we doubled over with an aching stomach? Maybe, it was the obvious hunger, or just the pure innocence of childhood rebellion. Never the less, it was all a part of the orchard in season. In any season, it was the best place to be when I was growing up. Quiet and serene, except for the sounds of laughter and the regular chatter of nature which remains to me an inspiration.

On my way to live in Europe with a successful husband and two beautiful, healthy daughters, this special place consumes my thoughts. "Why am I looking backward, instead of forward?" I wondered. That old creative restlessness was nudging me again. I wondered if this desire to write actually had something productive and lucrative attached to it, or was I just reminiscing about the childhood homestead as a way to escape the impending trip afar. I can only tell you that stress and change were my least preferred experiences in my youth.

We arrived in Rome on a very hot day, in June of 1994. I remember the temperature, not because we were sweltering, but because I was worried about our obese Chihuahua, Heidi. She had a medium sized kennel which we had placed a luxury cushion for her princess behind to sit on. If anything, the dog was not unlike our children which we pampered to the point of wreckage.

What goes wrong? It happens so quickly after those baby days and some of those cute toddler days. Then, before you know it they are in sixth or seventh grade refusing to get up for school. It is then that you realize what you have done or not done and are praying for God's mercy and grace.

I remember listening to a Christian radio show at that time. Someone asked the minister on the show, "You have four children and seemed to be doing very well, how do you do it?" He replied, "I pretend they are someone else's children." At the time, I didn't understand what he meant. It took me a few short weeks and I began to understand what he was saying.

Possibly he meant that he did not let their emotional meltdowns become his own. Less emotion, let's just get things done! I know I'm explaining it correctly because I pondered what he meant for some time afterwards and when I was able to act on his philosophy, it worked! When parents have too much emotion like frustration and anger, the parent's emotions will become the focus. The focus should be what the parents need for their children to do. I could still empathize with them, but it did not change what had to be done. Me, not melting down with them was of utmost importance. We experienced some raw, ugly moments, but we also benefitted from some wise teachings.

Long before I had any of this revelation, with my husband and two young children and doggie in tow, we arrived at the Costa Blue hotel in Penetimare, Italy. It would be our home for the next month or so. Located right by the water, which we could see from our sixth floor room. Wow! This was okay! Len and I agreed. Italy is six hours' time difference from the US and we all began to experience the fatigue. We were sleep deprived and hot, without A/C, but we attempted to settle in.

As nighttime approached, from the sixth floor up and an open terrace door, we could loudly hear the sounds of one of several discos in the area. Evidently, the Napolitano's love their disco's and dancing. Needless to say we woke-up, or were already awake when morning arrived.

The Timex watch boy, I mean, Len, went off to work already. The feeling of impending doom began to set in. Do I bolt the hell out of here or grab the nearest bottle of vino. This was momentary and I started to determine what we could do to pass the time. I put Erin in the stroller and the three of us visited the shops within walking distance. We ate gelato and bought kinder eggs. The girls were surprised with the small toy on the inside.

We located a nice villa in a "Parco" which was similar to a gated community in the US. The next three years we experienced the Italian culture, as well as German, French, and Slovenian cultures. It was an amazing experience. We minimally learned to speak some of the language, ate some glorious cuisine and experienced a beautiful camaraderie that Italians have for each other. It was memorable for all of us.

Len had some friends in Italy from a previous tour before we were married. The girls and I became friends with them too! Salvatore, Maria and their two children who were young adults by then. They became good friends. Len would come home and say, "Sal and Maria want to take us to a festa!" We would go up in the mountains and tour a little village where they had friends which of course would eventually end in a big feast. These were beautiful places, people, and food! It was always memorable. There were always children for Trish and Erin to play with. Sometimes other American families we knew would also go and the kids would all play together.

These were great memories, but not enough to stop what would ensue once the girls each hit 13. Pampering and a lack of teaching accountability at a young age, will not cultivate a good student or a motivated, interested adolescent. One of the main problems seems to be the soldier needs to be cultivated at a young age. Francis, my mother always did everything for the children when we were up to the age of eight or nine years old.

Len would say, "You pamper Trish too much." He wanted her to be more accountable. I learned the hard way, after going through the wreckage of teen hood with her and grew in wisdom. I felt Len, pampered Erin too much and I would always say she needed to be more accountable, don't you remember Trish? Then the scales fell from his eyes when Erin became a teenager, but it was too late.

The travel from Italy and living there for three years was beautiful, difficult, and a once in a lifetime experience. Len and I carried mostly good memories from our time in Europe, aside from the time I spent with my best amiga 'vino'. At times I would get drunk and it hurt those around me. I carried a lot of guilt from it. It wasn't a regular occurrence but certainly a demon that would come up along the way.

We moved back to the states. Being surrounded with the English language, regular running water, and electricity was to say the least, refreshing. Yippee! You know I must've been happy to be home when I agreed with Len to purchase a new Ford Taurus. Who cares! It was new and in America! In the land of the free! Not to say this is not a quality car, but my taste always tended to take the more expensive route. I guess Len was not aware that my previous repertoire of vehicles included a corvette. Regardless, I was joyful to be home and that was the most important thing now.

5   My Shaken Ground

The next few years back at home in the US, remained contentious between Len and I. Although his health seemed good, my emotional state ran hot or cold. Consistency was a difficult attribute for me to attain. My previous counseling taught me that the childhood stages people go through are progressive steps towards maturation and without successful maneuvering and the guidance of parents this is not accomplished very well. In essence I was growing up at the age of forty.

Reality can certainly bite! But the bite heals until you receive the next one. I do believe this might be for a while. Not until the end of time. The question is not how do I avoid the bite? But, how can I heal and recover quickly? Life does in fact bite frequently. This is in my experience and Len's. Do we need the faith that heals and the fellowship that comforts? This was our question. This is a question that Len and I had to come back to frequently.

The pastor of our church had a sermon that was about going around the same mountain over and over again. No truer words were spoken about a family before! This mountain path was so worn out that we had to construct a new one. But, I have to say, I was tired of this path and wanted off of it yesterday! The problem wasn't why can't we get off of it? I finally pinpointed a clear distinction between Len's goals for church and mine. Len wanted to show up for church on Sunday, say hi to everyone, and look forward to the next Sunday service. Now, there is nothing wrong with making it to church, tithing, and on occasion helping. He was perfectly content with this.

I knew I had a greater purpose that tied into my entire life story. For example, having a job affiliated with the church is like "killing two birds with one stone," for me. I wanted what I would do for a living (occupation) to reflect love and service to people and God (calling). This can be mostly any type of work, which I did not realize in the early days after returning to church. As time passed, my calling just seemed to make sense to me. My past issue of being unsafe and treated poorly reared its ugly head with every advance that I made. Talking about "no room for wimps," when it comes to changing for God the room is tight and like it says the path is narrow.

Through the beautiful teachings in scripture, I was able to grow in greater faith, prayer, and regular reading of the scripture. I was encouraged regularly. God gave me the strength to stop drinking once and for all. He became my best friend, instead of the wine. I had also tried "my" best to help out at church, but it never seemed to work out for one reason or another. I felt like no one would give me an opportunity. Was I too sensitive? Did they not like me, or judge me? Maybe I was too fearful of what people would think of me. It stemmed from guilt I felt. Rejection and guilt are two emotions the enemy will use to paralyze you with fear. I clung to scripture, reading and learning about the character of God. I learned what he wanted me to do and who he wanted me to be in his kingdom.

The relationships that I wanted to build, and the comfort that comes with knowing the hearts of others and being connected with them, seemed to elude me. Len was doing his usual things and perfectly content, but I knew the gifts that God created in me were for something more, something greater. Through many years of my young life, counseling had provided me with an understanding of my family dynamics and how I fit into that scheme. The pain was very heavy on my heart because the way that I fit in was to be shut out and blacklisted by the people I needed the most, my family.

As I write this at the age of fifty-one, I still feel my heart in pain from the past. I hold back the tears, suppressing for words instead. Words that will teach and heal myself and someone else, maybe you. What comes to my mind right now is, "Run Forest Run," but the running can't go on any longer. God needs me to be who he intended me to be for his kingdom. "If I perish, I perish," I think as I write. What is the worst thing that can happen from sharing my heart with you?

God is a loving God and his heart is for none of his children to perish. Sin is what makes people perish. God saw those who had sinned against me. God took that sin against me seriously. In His word, God states that he has come to seek justice and to return what was stolen from his children. I am his child and heir. He is faithful to return what the thief has stolen. This is a reason for thanksgiving! I am thankful to know this today. I can forgive those who hurt me because God is the righteous judge, not me.

When Trish was 13 we started to deal with issues of her running away. She was having sex, smoking cigarettes, and pot. I felt helpless. I really didn't know how to handle that situation. She was in and out of juvenile facilities and she tried a few times to overdose. I didn't understand what she was going through. Her boyfriend was 19 years old. She disappeared for over a month. When the police finally found her, I did what had to be done to keep her safe and requested she be sent to a teen help program in another state, far away. She had escaped once before from a local facility. That seemed to be our only hope.

We didn't see Trish for several months. I covered her in prayer daily. While she was at the program, she received Jesus as her savior and received the Holy Spirit. She was 17 when we drove her away from that place for good. She struggled with the pressure of peers and wanting a social life. She eventually would succumb to drugs and alcohol, but not before giving birth to a beautiful son, our first grandchild. One failed marriage (they were too young), and 3 more grandkids later, Trish is now a steadfast woman of God.

I saw my daughter completely delivered of addiction just like God delivered me of alcoholism. Now, instead of generational curses I have passed down generational blessings, because HE makes ALL things new! He who is in us is greater than he who is in the world! My past mistakes have been redeemed through Jesus Christ who makes all things work together for my good.

Len had to leave for Afghanistan for a few months. It was just Erin and I since Trish had her own place as an adult. I have to admit it was not my idea of a workable family life. I was trying to rise above the issue of parenting on my own for a few months, but I didn't seem to be rising as high as I think I "should." For me the word "should" spoken could cause me trouble. For example, I had a class in which the instructor gave me the wrong grade. I went to plead my case. I told him I believed I should have received an A on that exam! His reply to me was, "Should." I kid you not! That did happen. I did eventually get the earned grade, but found the experience a bit discouraging. Things will not always go as they "should." It is best for us to learn how to take it with stride when things don't go our way.

Our church attendance was pretty good except for the occasional illness or being "out of Towners." We strived to be committed, make regular tithes and catch-up tithes, if we were out of town. The sermons were excellent on a regular basis. I usually believed it was information I could put into use following the service or generally, in daily life. Improving on the daily quality of life was important to me because I it measures the fruit of the Holy Spirit at work in you. In other words, we must grow in faith through God's word and use it as a guide book. All things considered, I thought things in my life were progressing, but my experiences at church seemed to become rather discouraging.

One morning, the one after Len left, was an example of an odd occurrence. At least it seemed so to me. Worship, through singing, became my favorite experience in church. I was singing like a lark and a bit emotional, when the music just stopped. All I know is that the strong need to bolt out of there came across me, so I did. Fortunately, the service was nearing the end and it was not so obvious that I left early. Erin and I went to the Bob Evans for a little breakfast, but I carried this sense of heaviness on me. I knew the stress of the previous week working with Erin, who was now in sixth grade with clinical symptoms of ADHD was a huge challenge for me. She had great difficulty learning. It was a challenge to help even when Len was home, but when he was gone, it was even harder.

The weeks helping Erin and experiencing the stress of a child who is starting to get behind in school and struggling is a huge weight to carry. I continued to pray, the best I knew how. I encouraged, loved, and set boundaries for her daily. At times I really thought I was going to pass out from stress but I never did. I would talk to Len most days or at least every couple of days. The mood was tense. I constantly found myself wondering how to help her. What could I do differently? Why was my husband not available? I just was not at a place where I understood how to make a difference or solve this problem.

I hoped God could help me rise above it. I know that God could, but I did not know how to let him work in me that way yet. I would get so caught up in the stress of helping her, that I could not see my way to pray at times. I stopped going to church after that last experience and threw myself into Erin's problems.

I focused on my own school work frequently when she was at school. Getting the "C" I needed in college mathematics which includes upper level algebra and geometry was being brought along by my prayer and faith. I applied the sermons and scripture to my learning environment and tried to teach Erin to do this as well. I passed that course with the" C" I needed, because I gave it to God.

I always had a tendency to shut down from anxiety, when working on math in my youth and it continued right into my adulthood. So, when I was taking the final, (yeah, I made it to the final!), I started to go blank on the second page. When that happened, I began to pray. I asked God to keep my mind open and let everything I learned come out on the test and it did. I actually got a "B" on the test which for me was a major breakthrough!

I realized it was a matter of turning things that I struggled with over to him. If we do the foot work, he has the end result. It's a faith thing! I started to talk to Erin about this experience of mine and encouraged her that she could apply this too! We did see some improvements. She just had trouble receiving the faith.

I was really sad about having been away from church and I missed it greatly. Did anyone even know I had been bothered by something that last Sunday I had gone? Why did I feel the need to leave so suddenly? I decided my feelings were valid, although I didn't understand what caused them. I still determined to sit church out for a while.

I tried to maintain closeness to God through reading and prayer. It worked to some extent, but the knowledge, about the need for fellowship and attendance did bother me. I spoke with a lady from the church and we met a few times for breakfast. I viewed her as a mentor and tried to gain comfort and fellowship from our meetings. She encouraged me to come to church. At times I did, other times I would not go.

It was a time of shaken ground for me, and of not having a sense of knowing. I believed something literally chased me out of church that

Sunday. I could sense "it" but not see it. It was a little too much like the "twilight zone" in the making. I knew Len was going to be rubbing his head at this one. Maybe this could be overcome before he comes back home, like it never even happened? All I knew is that, for now, I could not go back to the church.

I wrote myself some "cosmic" letter about that Sunday since writing helps me to process my emotions and experiences. Many feelings that I experienced over those past four months seemed unusual, not something I had experienced previously. I even went as far as to share some of these with a local Psychologist. The question for me was, "Am I schizophrenic?" She laughed, and said, "Why is everyone so fearful of that diagnosis?" Then proceeded to tell me "no." I can't tell you how relieved I was! Was it depression, maybe? Could be, but what about not seeing things that were not there? I felt the attack so clearly but no comprehension of what it could be!

The fear of schizophrenia was based on some generational issues in my family. There were a variety of mental health issues. Why was my daughter's principal sitting in his truck, in the middle of the street? I came up in my van behind him and sat there for a minute or so. I was sure he saw us behind him. Maybe he had car trouble. Most occurrences and coincidences really do have a very simplistic explanation, for the most part. What about Erin's teacher, who on this same day, made faces at us in the parent teacher conference? Is that for real? I couldn't help but to feel the two things were connected in some way.

I had a great need for things to be accepted, for others to be friendly and caring. It caused me to experience a great deal of discomfort and rejection. Sometimes you just can't find a logical explanation for everything that happens and everyone's behavior. When you can't understand why you feel the way you feel and the lies of the enemy come in like a flood, who or what are you going to turn to? For me it was faith again. It was the only thing that could make sense to me. I began to read scripture more and to rely on God's word. I read a verse that talked about how he would keep us on solid ground and although my ground seemed pretty shaky, I began to experience a growing sense of faith. The ground was leveling!

5 Coming back to the heart

Len was happy to return from overseas and to have tempted fate one more time. It was a family condition passed from parent to child, a generational one. We needed a regular dose of excitement. Honestly, you could see it in Len's regular quest for road trips and work travel... Solutions one, attending interesting events, taking trips to different places of interest.

Unfortunately, I always had to be in charge of my own destiny. What did "I" learn? What was "MY" experience? Although my learning was of great importance, Len already had it figured out as ten years my senior, he had a few experiences I had not. Why was it so hard, for my hard head, to learn a valuable teaching from my husband Len? I think it had something to do with what he called himself when we first met: an 1890's man. It was 1990 at that time. Little did I realize that he was not joking. He had a high expectation of me as a homemaker, which fueled some resentment for me.

We had both lost loved ones, a fiancée for me, a spouse and two children for Len. Was it a coincidence that we found each other? I understood that God had a plan for our lives. One that is predetermined. Were we both so hard headed that we earned only the likes of each other? Now this was a good possibility!

Remember the radio broadcast that I had learned, "treating your children like they are someone else's?" I learned another bit of information that not only helped me but was beautiful and brought tears to my eyes. The pastor talked about "submission," actually the conversation came about through a caller on the radio. She talked about how she learned that the meaning of "submission" was to be under the safety and protection of someone. This was a far cry from the meaning I had in my mind of this word. I considered it to have mostly a negative meaning. I came from a background of distrust. My first thought was," you submit first, then I will." It must have been the right season, because I found this idea of safety, keeping each other safe, to be the most beautiful act of love. It redefined Christian love for me.

People did exist that I could trust! I finally experienced the freedom to submit, to be under the safety and care of those who love me. When we first started the faith journey back to church, learning to live according to scripture, my ability to experience love was very limited. I struggled to give it or receive it. It just was not a heartfelt, body and mind experience. I may have never received or felt that love before.

Out on an adventure in the orchard, where I grew up, I felt a sense of love for the freedom of the outdoors and its peacefulness. That was a great sense of freedom and wonder, but it was not the genuine feeling of a heart that is freed from anger, disappointment, and lack of forgiveness. The freedom in my heart is what I eventually began to experience in my faith walk. It was for one of the very first times, if ever, that I experienced real heartfelt empathy and compassion for my family or community.

Previously I always had some self-motivated factor involved. "How was this going to affect me?" "Do I have some personal reason to feel fear of harm in any way from this other person's decision?" To finally be set free of the concern over my safety was one of the most liberating experiences in my life.

To only think of how a situation affected someone else was a loving and lovely thing. I could only explain it as knowing what kind of love God wanted for us and comprehending how he looked at us through this single minded love. I'm not sure if I could of had a more significant spiritual revelation then this. But if there was one, I'd be ready. It radically changed my life.

Sometimes I think God places people around us to help us heal, like loving Christians who reach out to us no matter how fearful or hurt we are. A growing relationship with God will also bring into the light various things that need to be repaired in our life. When resentment exists with a spouse or family member, we need to heed the warning not to let the sun go down on our anger. Otherwise satan will get a foot hold and make it much worse.

    Len and I were like night and day. Whatever he chooses, it is certain, I will pick the other. We tested this. I thought he was just being oppositional, but it even happens when we are unaware of what the other chooses. It was confirmed, that we will need to work harder to stay united.

The word forgiveness pops up frequently. We will need to clear grudges and resentments from our life regularly. God cannot provide the blessings he has for us and intimacy with our spouse will become more and more obsolete without forgiveness. It's not necessarily that we "lose" love, it's that it gets covered over by the gunk, anger, and the un-forgiveness where hardens our hearts. God finds fault with us when we live in this way!

I really struggled the next year not seeing people I had become accustomed to in my church, but life went on with children and grandchildren. It was a busy life with Len. After the winter season that following summer we moved out west. Len was offered a lucrative job. It was an opportunity to leave a place that was filled with heartache from the many disappointments over the past ten years. Talk about guilt and condemnation! I was consumed with it most of those ten years feeling like a parental disaster.

After sending Trish away to school, her having a baby and getting married at 18, just to follow into drug addiction, and now Erin's school issues, we were at a loss. As my faith journey became stronger, God taught me that teens make choices and it is not necessarily due to bad parenting or lack of parenting. Although, we had fallen short, it was a good lesson learned not to live in condemnation, but grow by acknowledging any mistakes made.

We all take different approaches to our problems depending on who we are and our issues. I do know that for our children having absolutely no other option is what worked for them. For us that meant they had to be sent away to school where they had no other choices but to follow the rules there. By the time we understood how to discipline them, they were too old to receive it.

When Erin was 15, she was into the same things Trish had been, minus the running away. We sent her to a residential program as well. She also wound up discovering God while she was gone. One thing is for sure, my prayers were always interceding! God does answer prayer! She came home and later got lost again, like Trish, but in her own way. Today she also is a steadfast woman of God attending worship school at our church. I am so happy for what God has done for my children! He is faithful!

Today, I have faith that God is bringing us all along. We love our children and four grandchildren dearly. We remember the wisdom we have gained and apply it in our lives to the best of our ability. We remind our children and grandchildren, always, how they are loved. We encourage them to follow God's heart. As long as we are submitted to the Father, we are safe wherever he leads us and we remind ourselves of that daily.

Leading with the love of God that I have learned about in my life is what has healed me.

My children are very attentive and receptive when I am leading them in love (the fruit of the Spirit) and we usually pray together. We experience the presence of the Holy Spirit and healing takes place. The result is the presence of patience, faithfulness, and self-control in our family.

    Harder decisions lay ahead for us, as they do for every person. In Christ all things are possible. We learn to walk by faith and not by sight. That is how we, as followers of Jesus rise above the chaos. I carried a stronghold of rejection all my life. I ran away from fear of getting hurt. What I didn't realize is living that way hurts those around me and, myself. Living in fear empowers no one but the enemy of our soul.

With all I have been through, I know it at least served this purpose: that my testimony may encourage someone like you, not to live in the often paralyzing fear of rejection. Get out of the boat! If you want the blessings, you have to cast down every lie of the enemy and declare who you are in Christ!

You have to walk through to get on the other side. I do look back and reflect on what strides we have made. Forgiving yourself for not always having it right is in order. One-day consistency will kick in and sharing life together will get easier. It's like taking classes in college. You get to know your instructor and fellow students and it can be a good sense of camaraderie, but when it's over, it's over. When it is time to move on to the next level God's calling you to, you must go. The experience does not go away although the desire to continue in fellowship still exists. So how do you gain that community in your church? How do you gain it in your work place? Whether you go to a place of work, work at home, attend school or volunteer.

Today, I get the understanding that it's about finding a niche within that community to use the gifts God has anointed for you. I guess that's why spiritual gifts inventories are used by churches and the work place. After several years of taking these man made inventories of which, each one seemed a little different than the one before, I decided to pray and ask God himself what my gifts included.

Shortly after that I wrote a couple of poems. I made the mistake of showing them to my family of origin. I received sarcastic comments like, "Gee, you missed your calling" and "Oh, your sister can really write well!" Unfortunately, all the people you care about aren't going to support you in your God given gifts. Is it so difficult to give a little encouragement to one who is in need? Maybe so, but, I have felt that God is the one who will motivate me and he does. After all he is the one that answered my prayers leading me to write.

I believe it was on the Christian radio show when the minister, who was also a Psychologist, was discussing a book. He conveyed that whatever activity you engage in while experiencing the presence of the Holy Spirit might be an area of giftedness. My answer was to start singing mostly Christian music or something inspiring, that is usually a gift of the Spirit of God.

Within about a week's time I knew of two gifts God showed me that I was capable of. But it's not so easy to share with someone that you have these gifts. What if they don't agree? Once again, exposure to rejection, my struggle, reared its ugly head. The challenge is to be a God pleaser first.

I know that one day this challenge will be in the past and a new one will appear. This is regular living, at its best. We can count our blessings when a problem is no longer a problem. Deliverance comes from the Lord! God has to provide the grace, skills, and perseverance to rise higher. The best understanding, we can come to, is that the gifts we are blessed with need to be ignited on the inside by staying close to God. It is not about others as much it is about pleasing God. It is only about others because we are intended to use these gifts to help our hurting world. We are desperately needed, isn't that a great revelation!

This is a family journey we are on. It is amazing, painfully frustrating, and filled with blessings. It is by no means close to being over. We are in the midst of the love, the warfare, and confusion. The promises that God has made to us if we continue on and never give up, will surely come to pass. Whether it is the lack of forgiveness, lack of success in parenting, or the "False evidence appearing real" (fear), we can maintain a heart that knows real love. We can attend a church or build one, which teaches about God's love in action, through its members. If we experience love for others there, we can let this remind us that it is the greatest thing in life and it's the reason we existed to begin with. When it comes down to genuine love failure is not an option.

What does your journey look like today? What is your story of faith and what is God calling you to do? Sharing your story takes real faith! Stepping out in faith helps you see and hear the message God is giving you. I hope you will share your journey towards faith. God has a calling for each one of us and its time to get prepared for what it is.

nparsley@comcast.net

(e-mail your questions or stories).

Saving Faith: It is God's grace not our faith that saves us. In his mercy, however, when he saves us he gives us faith--a relationship with his son that helps us become like him.

Through the faith he gives us, he carries us from death into life (John 5:24, NLV)

-Inspired by God's calling-

Made in United States
Orlando, FL
13 September 2023